ALTERNATOR
BOOKS™

CREATE YOUR OWN BLOG

KAREN LATCHANA KENNEY

Lerner Publications ◆ Minneapolis

Lerner Publications Company
A division of Lerner Publishing Group, Inc.
241 First Avenue North
Minneapolis, MN 55401 USA

For reading levels and more information, look up this title at
www.lernerbooks.com.

Library of Congress Cataloging-in-Publication Data

The Cataloging-in-Publication Data for *Create Your Own Blog* is on file
    at the Library of Congress.
ISBN 978-1-5124-8343-7 (lib. bdg.)
ISBN 978-1-5124-8347-5 (EB pdf)

LC record available at https://lccn.loc.gov/2017014146

Manufactured in the United States of America
1-43345-33165-6/21/2017

CONTENTS

BE A BLOGGER!

DO YOU HAVE SOMETHING TO SAY? Blogging, short for weblogging, is a great way to share your latest obsession, deep thoughts, or unique view of the world. Whether it's about your robotics club or adventures in other countries, a blog lets you express what's on your mind and what you care about.

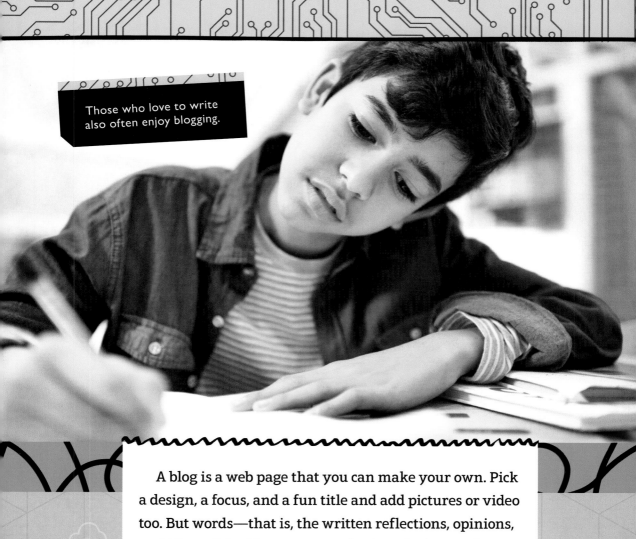

Those who love to write also often enjoy blogging.

A blog is a web page that you can make your own. Pick a design, a focus, and a fun title and add pictures or video too. But words—that is, the written reflections, opinions, and ideas of the blogger—are what's at the heart of most blogs. Just write new posts on a regular basis, and presto! You have a blog.

Your original work will reach readers close by or far away. You can connect with people who have similar interests as you and become a better blogger.

Are you ready to start blogging? Great—**LET'S GO!**

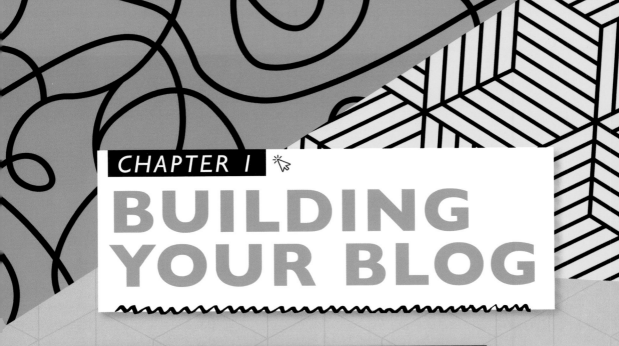

CHAPTER I
BUILDING YOUR BLOG

THE FIRST STEP TO BLOGGING IS FIGURING OUT WHAT YOU WANT TO SAY. Think of your blog's theme—this is the story you want to tell.

How do you pick? Ask yourself, what do I love? Maybe it's comic books, reggae music, or Halloween. Just start brainstorming, writing down everything that pops into your mind.

If you never tire of taking nature photos, then starting a nature blog might be up your alley.

Review your list and choose the most interesting topic. Picking a specific topic will attract an **audience** with similar tastes. If you like your topic a lot, you're going to want to keep creating new content that's related to that topic for a very long time.

Next, pick a fun title that reflects your blog's topic. Keep it short and catchy. It's the first hook to draw in your future readers.

CREATIVE TIP

Check out some blogs, and maybe one will inspire your blog's theme. Here are a few kinds you can create:

» **JOURNAL:** regular updates on life, a trip, a school project, or a special event

» **DIY:** step-by-step explanations of how to do things like knit a sweater, make spicy breakfast tacos, or create your own custom gift wrap

» **REVIEWS:** insights and opinions on books, movies, TV shows, and more

DIY blogs related to knitting are extremely popular. A web search for knitting blogs turns up more than nine hundred thousand results!

HIGH-TECH TOOLS

BLOGGING IS DONE ONLINE, OF COURSE, SO YOU NEED SOME TECHY TOOLS TO GET YOUR WORDS OUT THERE. Blog on a computer, tablet, or even a phone—you just need something you can type on. If you don't own one of these devices, visit a library and use its equipment.

A camera is necessary if you want to add photos and videos. You can use either a dedicated camera or a camera on a phone. Visuals can do more to explain an idea than words can do alone—plus, they're fun to look at.

Pick a **platform** to set up your blogging account and profile. Platforms are sites that host blogs. Be sure to ask a parent or guardian for help and permission first, as many sites require you to be at least thirteen to have a blog.

Some people like the convenience of blogging right from their phone.

LOOKING GOOD

 IT'S TIME TO CHOOSE A LOOK FOR YOUR BLOG.
Many platforms have free **templates** you can use.
Templates are designs that create the background for your
content. A design can look
simple or bold. It can be
colorful or black and white.
The choice is up to you!

Your blog's title goes in the
header, at the top of your
site. Some platforms let you
add an image there too, such
as a logo or a fun picture.
You also need to choose a
web address that readers
can use to access your site.

Photos are a big part of Truelane, a
popular fashion and lifestyle blog run by
fashion guru Chelsea Lankford (*right*).

ADORA SVITAK

Since she was four, Adora Svitak has been in love with words. She started writing short stories and blog posts at the age of seven. She's written several books too. In 2010 she gave a TED speech titled "What Adults Can Learn from Kids." More than four million viewers have seen it. As a young adult, Svitak continues to blog, writing for popular sites like *Huffington Post* and Mashable.

CHAPTER 2

CREATING GREAT POSTS

YOUR BLOG'S THEME IS THE BIG-PICTURE IDEA OF WHAT YOU WANT TO BLOG ABOUT. Posts are ways to discuss that theme. You can do this in many ways: through lists, interviews, stories, and more. You'll want to switch up the kinds of posts you write to keep things interesting.

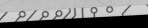

It can be helpful to bounce your ideas for posts off friends or family members.

A great way to come up with topic ideas is to brainstorm everything related to your theme. For example, if your theme is baking, you might make a list of all the things you can think of that have to do with baking: recipes, types of baked goods (cookies and bars, scones, biscuits, and more), favorite baking memories, the best dessert you ever made, and so on. Also, read all that you can about your topic—look in magazines, books, and online. Always be on the lookout for a good idea: at school, at home, and around town. Carry a notebook and a pen. Jot down your ideas before you forget, and soon you'll have a whole list of future posts.

Writers of all stripes, from novelists to bloggers, often keep a trusty notebook at the ready!

Some bloggers like to outline by putting pencil to paper before taking their ideas to a digital device.

Sitting in front of a blank screen can be intimidating. You've picked a topic for a post, but how do you write about it? Knowing the parts of a post can help you break writing down into manageable chunks. Make an **outline** as you think about each part of your post.

Volunteer to write for a school or neighborhood newspaper. You'll get to interview people, outline stories, and write and revise text too. No one is a great writer at first, but with each story you will improve. This kind of writing and editing experience is valuable and will likely make your blog better.

A post usually begins with a hook—the first few sentences that draw your reader in. They should be exciting and fun and should touch on what your post will be about. A good hook can be a question or an observation, a descriptive scene, or an explanation of how you connect with the topic.

Next are a few paragraphs about your topic. This is the body of your post, which covers the main ideas. Then include a good conclusion to wrap up your post. Summarize your thoughts and maybe address readers with a question to engage them more, encouraging them to leave comments.

IN DEPTH
ADDING IMAGES

An image can make a good post great. If you're writing about school lunches, take pictures of them. Use your own photos whenever possible. Other people own the pictures they took, and they may not want you using them. Anyone can use a **public domain** image, though. Here are two sites that have them:

- Pexels, https://www.pexels.com

- Pixabay, https://pixabay.com

Craft bloggers often like to take all the photos for their blog themselves. That way, they can show step-by-step photos of their crafts.

WRITE, READ, REVISE

→ **WITH YOUR OUTLINE DONE, YOU HAVE A PLAN TO FOLLOW AND YOU CAN BEGIN WRITING.**
Figure out when and where you like to write. Are early, quiet mornings best for you? A laptop on the couch might work, or an old-school pencil and notebook may be what you need.

Write your post out fully before posting it to your blogging platform, filling in each section of your outline as you go. This makes it easier to revise. You might opt to use a program that connects directly to your platform, such as Windows Live Writer. Keep your post short (about two hundred to three hundred words), and use an image, if needed, to explain your ideas.

Once you've written your post, read through it. Does it sound **conversational**? Does it make sense and follow your topic? Make sure your spelling and grammar check out. Revise the text, if needed, and then transfer it to your blogging platform. Don't hit Publish just yet—instead, save your text. You have just a few things left to do to create a truly polished post. But you're almost there!

CHAPTER 3

SHARING YOUR POSTS

BEFORE YOUR POST GOES LIVE, IT NEEDS A SHORT, CATCHY TITLE. A good title uses as few words as possible but says a lot about your topic. It's meant to grab a reader's attention quickly.

Catchy headlines get our attention both in print and online.

NIESE 49

NEW YORK

Mets win fifth straight to stay No. 1

HIGH 5!

BOSOX WITH 9-RUN SEVENTH: P. 48-49

How would *you* title a blog post about this school lunch?

Have fun with your title by using alliterations, series of words that begin with the same sound. Try "Friday's Funky Fish Sticks" instead of "The Bad Food I Ate on Friday." Which is more fun to say?

Another trick is to add bold words and interesting adjectives to your title. A bold word makes a strong statement, like *love*, *best*, and *brilliant*. Interesting adjectives describe subjects in engaging ways, like *weird*, *incredible*, or *curious*. Browse a thesaurus or a dictionary to find the perfect words to make your title pop.

Next, you'll want to add some **tags**, labels you add to a post that describe its content. Think of tags as words people might type in a search engine to find information on your topic.

Preview your post as a final check. A preview shows you what a post will look like online. Maybe the spacing between paragraphs looks off, or a photo isn't quite where you want it to be. You can fix these kinds of formatting issues after you've previewed your post.

Finally, publish your post. It can go live right away, or you can schedule it to go live later.

What about your next post? Decide how often you want to write for your blog. You'll need to post regularly, say once a week, to keep an audience interested.

When you're tagging your blog post, think about what you'd type into a search engine if you were looking for info on your post's topic. Whatever words you'd search for would make great tags.

MARLEY EMERSON DIAS

Dream of making a splash by sharing your writing online? Meet a girl who's done just that! In fact, eleven-year-old Marley Emerson Dias started her very own social media campaign. When Marley was looking for books to read, she noticed a big problem. She couldn't find many books featuring black girls, like herself. She started an online book drive to collect books about people of color. Books started pouring in! A year later, Marley had a deal to write a book about how other kids can make their dreams come true. Marley also shares her thoughts on her microblog on Twitter, giving insights into what's important to her, what she's reading, and what she's been up to.

GETTING READERS

YOU WANT YOUR POST TO BE READ, BUT HOW DO YOU ATTRACT AN AUDIENCE? Your tags might bring some readers to your blog, but there are other things you can do. Send an e-mail blast to friends and family. Let them know you have a new post online and provide a link to it. You can also announce your post on social media sites to spread the word.

Another great way to find readers is through other kids' blogs. Find ones that you like—maybe ones that are similar to yours. Leave comments on posts that you like, and add a link to your blog. That blog's readers might just want to check out yours.

Getting involved with a community of fellow bloggers—either online or off—can be a great way to build an audience for your blog.

Keep a list of the blogs you like. Add links to those blogs on your site's home page. You can help another blogger get a bigger audience. Maybe that blogger will add a link to your site on their blog. It'll help your audience grow too!

List the names of favorite blogs on a digital device or on good old-fashioned paper. Then you can add links to them on your blog.

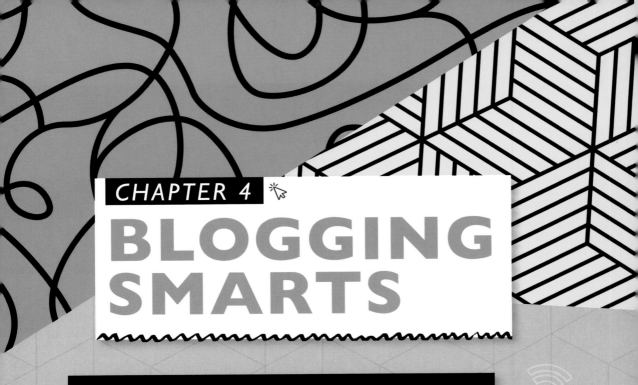

CHAPTER 4

BLOGGING SMARTS

BLOGGING CAN BE REALLY PERSONAL: YOU SHARE YOUR THOUGHTS, EXPERIENCES, AND PICTURES. But you don't really know who's reading what you write.

That's why you need to protect yourself. If you aren't comfortable having a public blog, you can limit who can read your posts. Check the privacy settings on your blog. You can approve only certain users, making your blog invisible to the public.

☟ IN DEPTH

PERMANENT

POSTS

What you write goes out to many readers, and a post is permanent—unless, of course, you decide to delete it. Don't use your blog to bash other people and promote negative ideas. **Cyberbullying can have devastating effects on others. Spread positive messages instead. You'll want that kind of positivity to have a permanent place on your blog.**

Bullying is never OK, whether in real life or online.

If you do make your blog public, don't provide personal details. Never give out your full name or birthday. Use a pseudonym—a fake name that authors use—and don't post pictures of yourself, your family, or your friends.

When you post your words on a public blog, you become part of a larger community. If you choose to, you can interact with that community by allowing readers to comment on your posts. If you aren't sure you want every comment you get to go live, you have the option to screen those comments and choose which ones to publish.

You can and should delete any rude or bullying comments others leave on your blog.

Blogs inspire others who share your interests, from bakers and knitters to adventurers and nature lovers.

Thank readers for their comments and answer their questions—it keeps the conversation going. An honest **critique** may be hard to take, but don't just dismiss it. You might be able to use some of a reader's advice to improve your blog. But if someone is unnecessarily negative, just delete the comment.

You officially know the basics of creating your own blog. As you sprint ahead in your blogging adventure, just remember to have fun, be creative, and stay true to yourself! Soon you'll see your words reach and inspire others.

BLOG CHECKLIST

ARE YOU READY TO GET YOUR NEW BLOG UP AND RUNNING? Here's a list of the basic tasks you'll need to accomplish. Use it to set up your blog and publish posts.

1. Decide what you want your blog's theme to be. Think of what interests you the most, so you'll stay inspired to write.

2. Find the equipment you'll need to start your blog. You'll need access to a computer, tablet, or smartphone. Find a camera you can use as well (a camera phone will do just fine) so that you can add photos and videos to your posts.

3. Get permission from a parent or guardian, and then set up a blogging account and profile.

4. Make your blog look good by choosing a design template.

5. Create a fun title for your blog, and place it in the header on your site.

6. Decide what kinds of pages you want on your blogging site and add them. Create content to fill the non-post pages.

7. Brainstorm topics that relate to your theme. Pick the best ones to use as your future posts.

8. Choose one topic to write about for a post, and create an outline.

9. Find a good time and place to write—in the morning on your laptop or on a notebook in the park or however you like. Then write your post. Just let the words flow.

10. Revise your post, changing the parts that don't work or sound awkward. Also check spelling and grammar. You can ask a friend or family member to read it too.

11. Give your post a catchy title, and add an image or two. Tag the post with relevant labels.

12. Preview your post, and adjust it if the formatting is off.

13. Publish your post. Now readers can enjoy learning about your latest adventure, delicious new recipe, or science project.

14. Keep thinking of new topics and write regularly. Regular posts keep an audience interested.

GLOSSARY

audience: the people who read a blog

conversational: a casual style of writing that reads like the way a person speaks

critique: an examination or judgment of something

cyberbullying: bullying someone electronically—for example, posting mean messages about a person

header: information at the top of a document or web page

outline: a plan of the basic points or ideas a person wants to write about

platform: the software or service a person chooses to blog on

public domain: not owned by a particular person and free for anyone to use

tags: labels attached to a blog or post that help others search for its content

templates: designs that a blogger can choose to use for a blogging site

Expand learning beyond the printed book. Download free, complementary educational resources for this book from our website, www.lerneresource.com.

FURTHER INFORMATION

Birley, Shane. *How to Be a Blogger and Vlogger in 10 Easy Lessons.* Lake Forest, CA: Walter Foster Jr., 2016.

Elle Special Edition 'Zine by Marley Dias
http://www.elle.com/marleymag

Fontichiaro, Kristin. *Blog It!* Ann Arbor, MI: Cherry Lake, 2012.

Kenney, Karen Latchana. *David Karp: The Mastermind behind Tumblr.* Minneapolis: Lerner Publications, 2013.

Krasner, Barbara. *12 Great Tips on Writing a Blog.* Mankato, MN: 12-Story Library, 2016.

Lindeen, Mary. *Digital Safety Smarts: Preventing Cyberbullying.* Minneapolis: Lerner Publications, 2016.

TED: Adora Svitak—"What Adults Can Learn from Kids"
https://www.ted.com/talks/adora_svitak

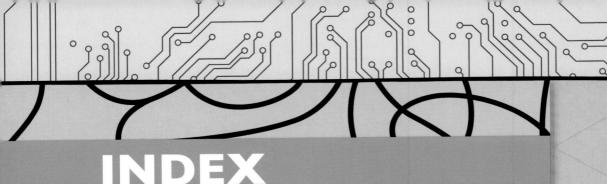

INDEX

PHOTO ACKNOWLEDGMENTS

The images in this book are used with the permission of: design elements: iStock.com/Sylverarts; iStock.com/chaluk; iStock.com/pixaroma; Iliveinoctober/Shutterstock.com; iStock.com/chekat; iStock.com/slalomp; iStock.com/ulimi; iStock.com/fonikum; content: AlesiaKan/Shutterstock.com, p. 4; iStock.com/PeopleImages, p. 5; Anton_Ivanov/Shutterstock.com, p. 6; iStock.com/Imgorthand, p. 7; iStock.com/Floortje, p. 8; iStock.com/RapidEye, p. 9; McClatchy-Tribune/Tribune Content Agency LLC/Alamy Stock Photo, p. 10; Sportsfile/Getty Images, p. 11; iStock.com/asiseeit, p. 12; iStock.com/fstop123, p. 13; iStock.com/kali9, p. 14; iStock.com/sbossert, p. 16; New York Daily News/Getty Images, p. 18; iStock.com/kcline, p. 19; Evan Lorne/Shutterstock.com, p. 20; Steve Granitz/WireImage/Getty Images, p. 21; Rawpixel.com/Shutterstock.com, p. 22; iStock.com/Photo_Concepts, p. 23; iStock.com/dorioconnell, p. 24; iStock.com/Highwaystarz-Photography, p. 25; iStock.com/monkeypics, p. 26; iStock.com/AVAVA, p. 27 (girl baking); iStock.com/PeopleImages, p. 27 (boy camping).

Front cover: LWA/Dann Tardif/Blend Images/Getty Images.